FIRST 50 RIFFS

YOU SHOULD PLAY ON GUITAR

Tips written by Michael Mueller

ISBN 978-1-5400-2825-9

Visit Hal Leonard Online at
www.halleonard.com

Contact us:
Hal Leonard
7777 West Bluemound Road
Milwaukee, WI 53213
Email: info@halleonard.com

In Europe, contact:
Hal Leonard Europe Limited
42 Wigmore Street
Marylebone, London, W1U 2RN
Email: info@halleonardeurope.com

In Australia, contact:
Hal Leonard Australia Pty. Ltd.
4 Lentara Court
Cheltenham, Victoria, 3192 Australia
Email: info@halleonard.com.au

CONTENTS

Ain't Talkin' 'Bout Love

Words and Music by Edward Van Halen, Alex Van Halen, Michael Anthony and David Lee Roth

ARTIST: Van Halen

ALBUM: *Van Halen*

YEAR: 1978

GUITARIST: Eddie Van Halen

TIP: This riff is essentially arpeggiated notes of the underlying chords (Am–F–G5). As such, you'll want to finger the full open chord shapes on each change. For the G5, make sure you're playing the low G note with your fret hand's 2nd finger, which you'll immediately shift over to the C note on the 5th string.

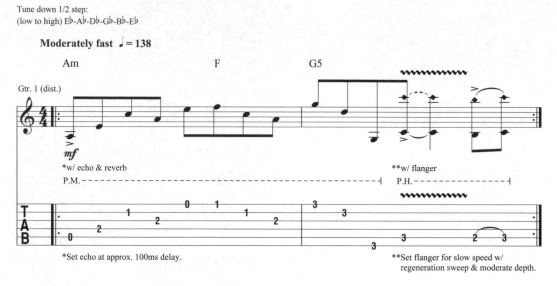

All Right Now

Words and Music by Andy Fraser and Paul Rodgers

ARTIST: Free

ALBUM: *Fire and Water*

YEAR: 1970

GUITARIST: Paul Kossoff

TIP: The barre-chord version of an open A chord is the anchor for this riff. For the opening A5, you'll add your pinky on strings 2–1 at the 5th fret. Then remove the pinky, maintain the A-chord barre, and add your 2nd finger at the 3rd fret on string 2 and your ring finger at the 4th fret on string 4, for the D/A. For the Dadd4/9, repeat the D/A motion, but then lift the barre, allowing the open G and E strings to ring.

Aqualung

Words and Music by Ian Anderson and Jennie Anderson

ARTIST: Jethro Tull

ALBUM: *Aqualung*

YEAR: 1971

GUITARIST: Martin Barre

TIP: This all-time classic riff is constructed from the G blues scale (G–B♭–C–D♭–D–F) and is played in 3rd position; that is, place your index finger at the 3rd fret, middle finger at the 4th, ring finger at the 5th, and pinky at the 6th. From there, you'll use all four fingers—one per fret—to execute the riff. Use strict alternate picking, beginning with an upstroke on the opening 5th-fret D note.

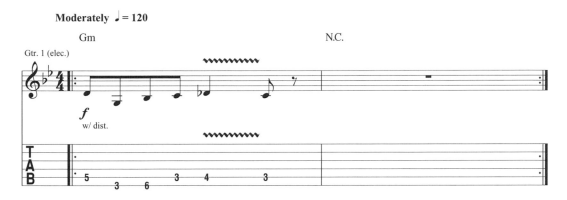

Are You Gonna Go My Way

Words by Lenny Kravitz
Music by Lenny Kravitz and Craig Ross

ARTIST: Lenny Kravitz

ALBUM: *Are You Gonna Go My Way*

YEAR: 1993

GUITARIST: Lenny Kravitz

TIP: Kravitz's blues influences are on full display here, with an open-position minor pentatonic riff in E, from the same gene pool as classics by Muddy Waters, John Lee Hooker, and others. Use your fret hand's middle finger for all the notes on the 2nd fret, including the bends. For the G/D double stop at the 3rd fret, use your ring and pinky fingers on strings 2 and 1, respectively.

Back in Black

Words and Music by Angus Young, Malcolm Young and Brian Johnson

ARTIST: AC/DC

ALBUM: *Back in Black*

YEAR: 1980

GUITARIST: Angus Young, Malcolm Young

TIP: Rhythm is king here, as the rests are just as important as the notes and chords. The descending lick comes straight out of the E minor pentatonic scale (E–G–A–B–D), and should be played with your ring finger for all 3rd-fret notes and middle finger for all 2nd-fret notes. For the syncopated climb that closes the riff, use your index finger for the 5th-string B note, and your ring finger for each note on the 6th string—the way Malcolm did it. Alternatively, you can switch to your pinky for the stretch from frets 5–7.

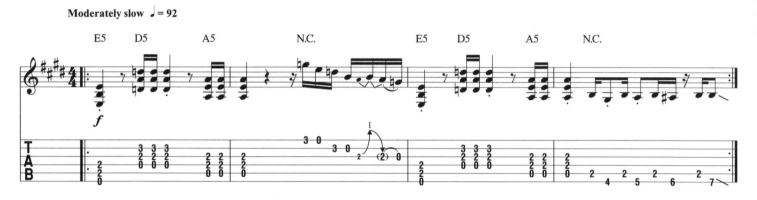

Barracuda

Words and Music by Nancy Wilson, Ann Wilson, Michael Derosier and Roger Fisher

ARTIST: Heart

ALBUM: *Little Queen*

YEAR: 1977

GUITARISTS: Howard Leese, Roger Fisher

TIP: The "horse gallop" rhythm on the open E5 chord in this riff is one of the most popular rhythm guitar devices in hard rock and heavy metal. Use a downstroke on the downbeat and the first of the 16th notes with an upstroke on the second 16th in each beat, and repeat. The harmonics are of the "open" variety. Lightly touch the strings *directly over the indicated frets* and strum to get that bell-like chime.

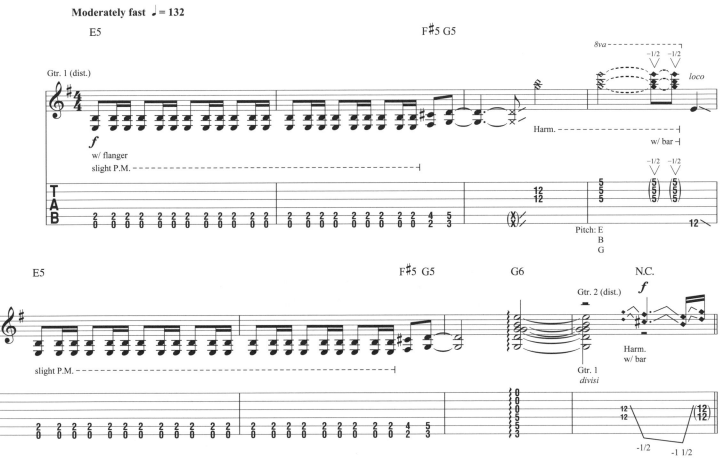

Born Under a Bad Sign

Words and Music by Booker T. Jones and William Bell

ARTIST: Albert King

ALBUM: *Born Under a Bad Sign*

YEAR: 1967

GUITARISTS: Albert King, Steve Cropper

TIP: Though the riff looks like it's operating out of an E major pentatonic pattern, it's actually built from its relative C# minor pentatonic scale (C#–E–F#–G#–B). Start the riff with your fret hand's ring finger on the F# on the 6th string, and then slide it up to the G# and the rest falls under a very natural fingering pattern. Watch that 1/4-step bend on the 4th string. That little nudge, from the minor 3rd (E) to a place between that and the major 3rd (E#), is a defining sound of the blues.

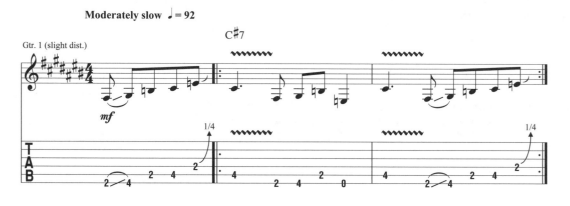

Brain Stew

Words by Billie Joe Armstrong
Music by Green Day

ARTIST: Green Day

ALBUM: *Godzilla* (Motion Picture Soundtrack)

YEAR: 1998

GUITARIST: Billie Joe Armstrong

TIP: This riff is fueled, tonally, by a wall of distortion, so your palm-muting technique needs to be on point. Immediately following a double downstroke, clamp your palm down on the strings to ensure silence during the rests. Use your index, ring, and pinky fingers on strings 6, 5, and 4, respectively for the A5, G5, F#5, and F5 power chords, and a 1st-finger barre on strings 5 and 4 for the E5.

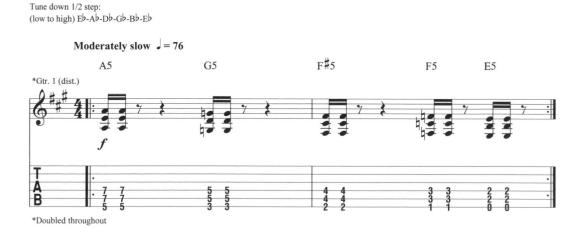

Brown Eyed Girl

Words and Music by Van Morrison

ARTIST: Van Morrison

ALBUM: *Blowin' Your Mind*

YEAR: 1967

GUITARISTS: Eric Gale, Hugh McCracken, Al Giorgioni

TIP: This opening double-stop riff is a veritable lesson in harmonizing 3rds intervals. For shapes over the G chord, use a first-finger barre on strings 2–3 at the 12th fret, then your middle and ring fingers on the 2nd and 3rd strings, respectively, for the next two double stops. For the C chord, use your index and middle fingers on strings 1 and 2, respectively, for the first shape, and then the index and ring fingers for the next two.

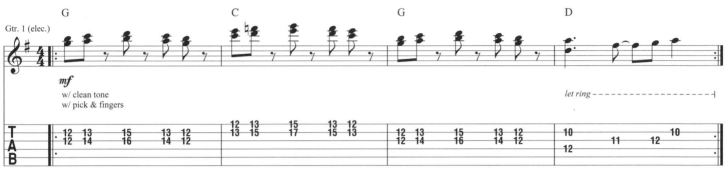

Carry on Wayward Son

Words and Music by Kerry Livgren

ARTIST: Kansas

ALBUM: *Leftoverture*

YEAR: 1976

GUITARISTS: Kerry Livgren, Rich Williams

TIP: Believe it or not, you only need two fingers to play this classic American prog rock riff. Start with your fret hand's ring finger for the quick grace note slide from the 4th to the 5th fret. Your ring finger will continue to play the rest of the notes on the 5th fret while your index finger will manage the notes at the 3rd fret. In bar 2, you'll slide the shape up two frets briefly. For the rapid descent on beat 4, fret the 7th-fret E with your ring finger, the 5th-fret D with your index, and then shift that back down to the 3rd-fret C. The only other hitch is the 2nd-fret F# at the end of bar 3, for which you can just stretch your index finger back a bit to grab.

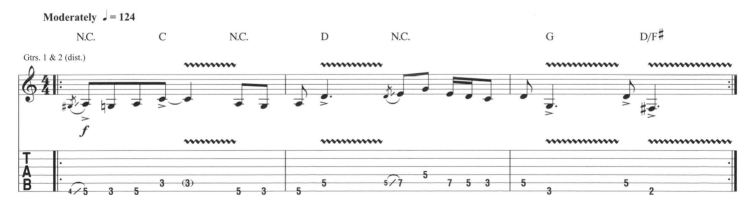

Come as You Are

Words and Music by Kurt Cobain

ARTIST: Nirvana

ALBUM: *Nevermind*

YEAR: 1991

GUITARIST: Kurt Cobain

TIP: This wily riff employs a very efficient single-note phrase to imply the underlying F#m–E5 harmony. You'll play this in open position using only your first and second fret-hand fingers. Note that Cobain's guitar was tuned down a whole step, to D, for this tune, but for our purposes, there's no need to detune unless you want to play along with the original recording.

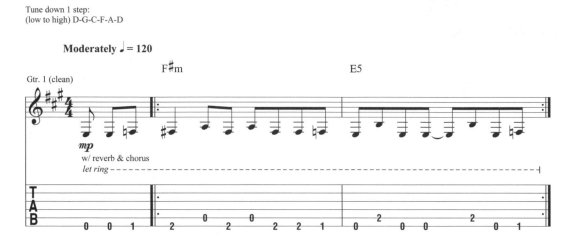

Crazy Train

Words and Music by Ozzy Osbourne, Randy Rhoads and Bob Daisley

ARTIST: Ozzy Osbourne

ALBUM: *Blizzard of Ozz*

YEAR: 1981

GUITARIST: Randy Rhoads

TIP: *All Aboard!* Randy Rhoads left an indelible mark on rock and metal guitar, none greater than the timeless opening riff to "Crazy Train." Played in 2nd position, the riff comprises notes from the F# minor scale (F#–G#–A–B–C#–D–E), and features *pedal point* technique, where notes are played alternately against the low F# note in measure 1 and against the B note in measure 2. You can use alternate picking for efficiency, but also try using all downstrokes, like Randy did.

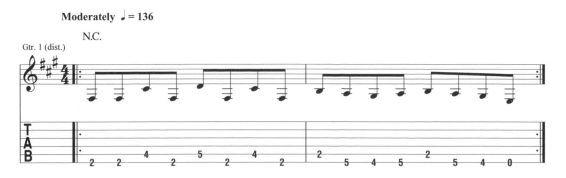

Do I Wanna Know?

Words and Music by Alex Turner

ARTIST: Arctic Monkeys

ALBUM: *AM*

YEAR: 2013

GUITARISTS: Jamie Cook, Alex Turner

TIP: The two key elements to executing this sober riff true to form are smoothly nailing the grace-note hammer-ons throughout, and properly timing the phrase that begins on the final 16th note of bar 2. You'll be tempted to play that Bb on the "and" of beat 4, but you need to be patient and wait that extra 16th note.

Don't Fear the Reaper

Words and Music by Donald Roeser

ARTIST: Blue Öyster Cult

ALBUM: *Agents of Fortune*

YEAR: 1976

GUITARISTS: Donald "Buck Dharma" Roeser, Eric Bloom

TIP: At first glance, this riff looks pretty easy, but making the chord changes "in time," keeping a steady eighth-note rhythm, and getting the open G to sound cleanly immediately after the fretted A note on beat 2 of bar 1 will all take a bit of practice. For the A5, use your middle finger on E and ring finger on A; for G, use your middle on B and ring on G; and for the F chord, your index on F and ring finger on C. Also, use downstrokes throughout, except for an upstroke on every open G string note.

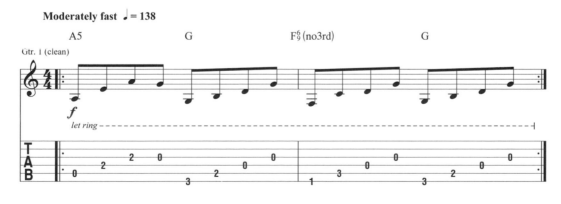

Enter Sandman

Words and Music by James Hetfield, Lars Ulrich and Kirk Hammett

ARTIST: Metallica

ALBUM: *Metallica* (Black Album)

YEAR: 1991

GUITARISTS: James Hetfield, Kirk Hammett

TIP: The key for making all the notes in this riff ring cleanly is in the left-hand fingerings. Keep your index finger planted on the 4th string, 5th fret, and your pinky anchored on the 5th string, 7th fret. Then use your ring finger on the 6th string, 6th fret, and your middle finger for the note that follows on the 5th fret.

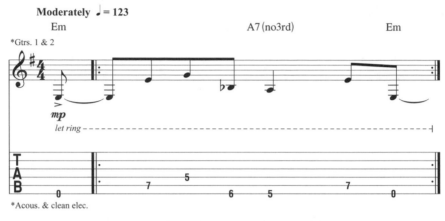

Iron Man

Words and Music by Frank Iommi, John Osbourne, William Ward and Terence Butler

ARTIST: Black Sabbath

ALBUM: *Paranoid*

YEAR: 1971

GUITARIST: Tony Iommi

TIP: Although this riff features a single, movable power-chord shape, there are a couple of potential speed bumps. First, note that there are two types of slides in this riff: one where you strum the target chord and one where you don't. If the slide has a curved "slur" symbol, you do *not* strum the target chord. Second, because you're playing power chords as high up on the neck as the 15th fret, it's best to finger the power chords with your index and ring fingers.

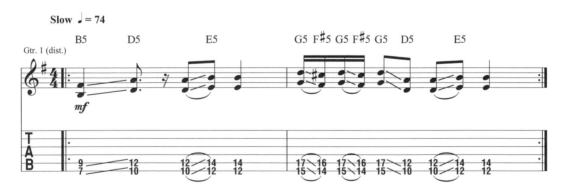

Jumping Jack Flash

Words and Music by Mick Jagger and Keith Richards

ARTIST: Rolling Stones

ALBUM: *Hot Rocks 1964–1971*

YEAR: 1968

GUITARISTS: Keith Richards, Brian Jones

TIP: The Rolling Stones have played "Jumping Jack Flash" more than any other song in the band's monumental catalog. Keith uses a capo at the 2nd fret. Play the tab as if the capo were the nut. Your index finger will take care of the fretting duties.

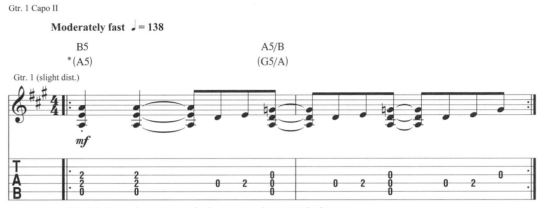

*Symbols in parentheses represent chord names respective to capoed guitar.
Symbols above reflect actual sounding chords. Capoed fret is "0" in tab.

Killing in the Name

Written and Arranged by Rage Against The Machine

ARTIST: Rage Against the Machine

ALBUM: *Rage Against the Machine*

YEAR: 1993

GUITARIST: Tom Morello

TIP: The first thing you need to do before playing this crafty riff is tune your 6th string down a whole step, to D. As a result, you'll be playing power chords with a single-finger barre on the lowest two strings; index for the E5, middle for the F5. For the muted strums, indicated by "x" in the transcription, you need to lay both your middle and ring fingers across the strings with enough pressure to mute the strings but not so much that you accidentally fret notes. The reason for using both fingers is to help avoid sounding harmonics.

La Bamba

By Richard Valenzuela

ARTIST: Ritchie Valens

ALBUM: *Ritchie Valens*

YEAR: 1959

GUITARIST: Ritchie Valens

TIP: A classic chordal riff, Valens exploited dyads pulled from the open chord shapes of C, F, and G, creating melody and harmony all at once, along with single-note runs reminiscent of the country guitar legend Mother Maybelle Carter. As such, you'll want to apply those open chord shapes as you play this riff, but making sure to play just the dyads. Start the opening bass-line phrase with your fret hand's ring finger on G and ending it with that same finger on C, while forming the C chord along with it. Simply, if you assign one finger per fret, it should all go smoothly.

La Grange

Words and Music by Billy F Gibbons, Dusty Hill and Frank Lee Beard

ARTIST: ZZ Top

ALBUM: *Tres Hombres*

YEAR: 1973

GUITARIST: Billy Gibbons

TIP: You'll need only two fret-hand fingers to play a majority of this fast Texas shuffle from the great Reverend Willy G., as Gibbons is also known—your index finger holds a barre at the 2nd fret on strings 4–3 throughout, and your pinky finger finds those 5th fret G and C notes in measure 2. You'll use your middle finger to fret the C-to-A pull-off on beat 3 of the 4th bar, followed by your pinky on the 5th fret D note. The tricky part in playing this riff is using *hybrid picking*; that is, using your pick and fingers to pluck the strings. Here, you'll pluck all notes on strings 4–3 with your pick hand's middle and ring fingers, respectively, and you'll use your pick on the open 5th string.

Layla

Words and Music by Eric Clapton and Jim Gordon

ARTIST: Derek and the Dominoes

ALBUM: *Layla and Other Assorted Love Songs*

YEAR: 1970

GUITARISTS: Eric Clapton, Duane Allman

TIP: Not enough can be said about solid technique. In order to properly reproduce the energy of this iconic riff, it's important to play each hammer-on, pull-off, and bend cleanly and precisely. For the whole-step bends on the 13th and 15th frets, use either your pinky or ring finger, making sure to place your remaining left-hand fingers on the frets behind the one being bent to add support and make the full whole-step bends easier to accomplish.

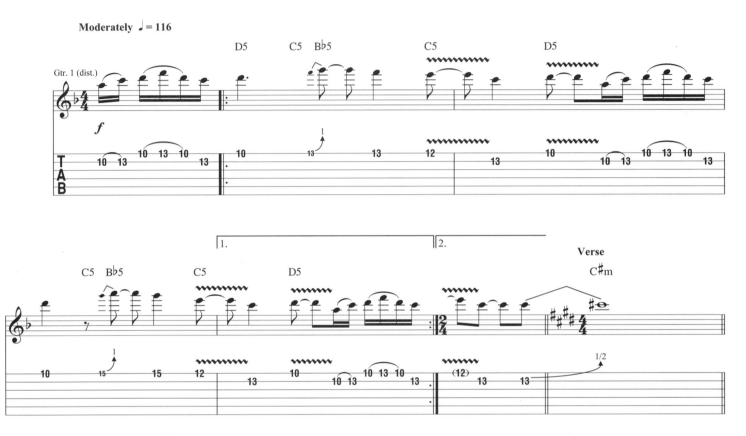

Life in the Fast Lane

Words and Music by Don Henley, Glenn Frey and Joe Walsh

ARTIST: Eagles

ALBUM: *Hotel California*

YEAR: 1976

GUITARISTS: Joe Walsh, Don Felder

TIP: This four-bar riff features several essential rock moves and compositional devices. The main theme is stated in bar 1. The phrase formed by the first five notes has served as a launching pad for myriad rock guitar licks. You'll play the 7th-fret notes on strings 5–4 using a "rolling" technique, where you place your ring finger across both strings, but sort of "roll" the downward pressure from string to string as needed. Bar 2 restates the main theme, but doesn't resolve to the root, E. Bar 3 restates the theme from bar 1, but then employs a device called *rhythmic displacement*—here, moving the first two notes of the main theme from the downbeat of bar 4 instead to the final two 16th notes in bar 3, to give it a time-shifting feel.

Message in a Bottle

Music and Lyrics by Sting

ARTIST: The Police

ALBUM: *Regatta de Blanc*

YEAR: 1979

GUITARIST: Andy Summers

TIP: Built on a progression of suspended 2nd chords (sus2), "Message in a Bottle" is a textbook example of Andy Summers' guitar style. To begin, fret the C#sus2 with your index, ring, and pinky fingers on strings 5, 4, and 3, respectively. Now that you've got that shape, you're just going to move it around the fretboard, shifting to string set 6–4 for the final three chords. Note that you do *not* have to place all three fingers in place before playing the first note of each chord; however, keep your fingers down for the duration of each chord before going onto the next, so the notes ring together as much as possible.

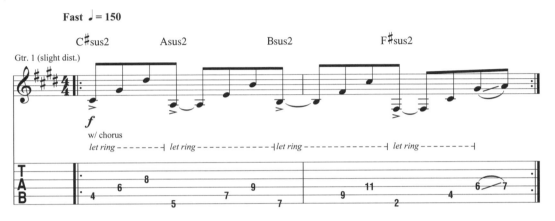

Mission: Impossible Theme

from the Paramount Television Series MISSION: IMPOSSIBLE
By Lalo Schifrin

COMPOSER: Lalo Schifrin

ALBUM: *Mission: Impossible* (Soundtrack)

YEAR: 1967

TIP: Though originally not a guitar riff, the "Mission: Impossible" theme is nonetheless very popular among guitarists. The riff is in 5/4 time; that is, there are five beats per measure, each with the value of a quarter note. You count this as: *one, two, three, four, five.* The famous two-bar theme at the beginning is played in 1st position. For the flute part in bars 3–6, shift up to 3rd position.

Money for Nothing

Words and Music by Mark Knopfler and Sting

ARTIST: Dire Straits

ALBUM: *Brothers in Arms*

YEAR: 1985

GUITARIST: Mark Knopfler

TIP: Guitarist Mark Knopfler plays this riff—as well as all his others—fingerstyle, and although you *can* play it with a pick, you won't get the same effect and tone, so let your pick hand's thumb, index, and ring finger do the talking. The easy rule of thumb, so to speak, is that you'll use your thumb to play all the notes on string 4, *except* for when the dyads fall on strings 5–4, in which case your thumb plucks string 5. Other key elements include the 5th-fret harmonic in bar 5, and the 4th-fret one in bar 7. Lightly touch the string directly over the fretwire and pluck to sound the harmonic.

Monkey Wrench

Words and Music by David Grohl, Nate Mendel and Georg Ruthenberg

ARTIST: Foo Fighters

ALBUM: *The Colour and the Shape*

YEAR: 1997

GUITARISTS: Dave Grohl, Pat Smear

TIP: The main riff in this song features a melody along the G string while the top two strings ring open. For this part, use just your middle finger to slide along the G string, always looking to the next note you need to hit rather than the one you're playing, to help ensure greater accuracy. The Drop D tuning legend and the chord symbols above the music pertain to the rhythm guitar power chords, which provide a firm foundation for this riff.

Drop D tuning:
(low to high) D-A-D-G-B-E

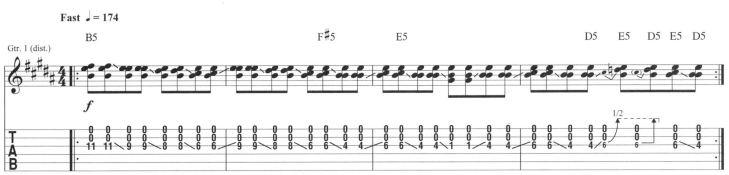

More Than a Feeling

Words and Music by Tom Scholz

ARTIST: Boston

ALBUM: *Boston*

YEAR: 1976

GUITARIST: Tom Scholz

TIP: The single-note arpeggios in this riff should flow smoothly, and the best way to accomplish this is to pay attention to the chord symbols above the tab. For the Dsus4, place your first finger on the 2nd fret of string 3, ring finger on the 3rd fret of string 2, pinky on the 3rd fret of string 1, and middle finger right behind the pinky on the 2nd fret of string 1. It might seem strange to have two fingers on the same string at the same time but doing this will allow you to simply remove the pinky in order to switch to the D chord on beat two of measure 1. Leave your ring finger down on the 3rd fret of string 2 for the entire riff. In measure 2, this naturally leaves your middle finger to play the 3rd fret on strings 5 and 6 and your index finger to play the 2nd fret on string 5.

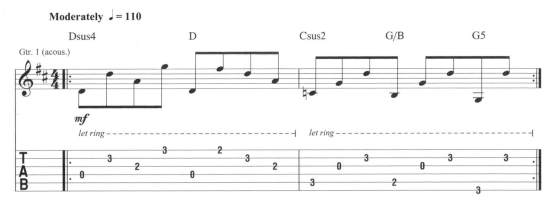

No One Knows

Words and Music by Mark Lanegan, Josh Homme and Nick Oliveri

ARTIST: Queens of the Stone Age

ALBUM: *Songs for the Deaf*

YEAR: 2002

GUITARIST: Josh Homme

TIP: To cop this stoner-rock riff, you first need to tune your entire guitar down *two* whole steps, to C standard: C–F–B♭–E♭–G–C. Next, form an open Am chord, slide it up to the 8th fret, and then place your pinky finger on the 2nd string at the 10th fret, while keeping your index finger down on the 8th fret. You're now in position to play this riff. However, it's a good bet that your strings are rather slack in this tuning, unless you use a heavy gauge. If the slack is too severe, you can return to standard E tuning, but keep the 6th string tuned down to C. Then, move that Am chord shape back to the 4th fret and play the riff.

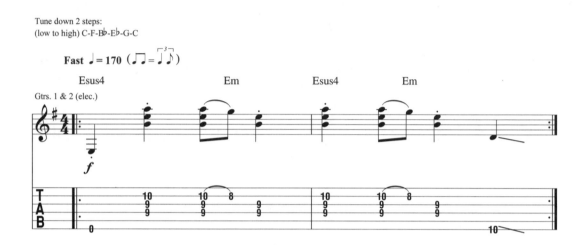

Oh, Pretty Woman

Words and Music by Roy Orbison and Bill Dees

ARTIST: Roy Orbison

ALBUM: *Orbisongs*

YEAR: 1965

GUITARISTS: Roy Orbison, Jerry Kennedy

TIP: Formed from the E major pentatonic scale (E–F#–G#–B–D), Orbison's "Oh, Pretty Woman" riff has proven timeless over the past 50-plus years. Though it begins with two open low E notes, your fret hand sits in 2nd position (index finger at the 2nd fret). It's a very simple riff, with the only issue being whether to use alternate (down-up-down-up) picking or all downstrokes. To be quite honest, it doesn't really matter; use whichever technique is most comfortable for you.

Outshined

Words and Music by Chris Cornell

ARTIST: Soundgarden

ALBUM: *Badmotorfinger*

YEAR: 1991

GUITARIST: Kim Thayil

TIP: This grunge-era riff is set in drop-D tuning (D–A–D–G–B–E), which allows you to play all the power chords with a one-finger barre shape. Use all downstrokes and be sure to lightly rest your palm on the strings, near the bridge, while picking the open D5 chords that start the riff. Use your fret hand's index finger for the F5 and your ring finger for the G5, as well as for the A♭5 later in the riff, shifting it down one fret to grab the G5 on the way down. Note, too, that the riff is in 7/4 time, which means there are seven quarter-note beats per measure.

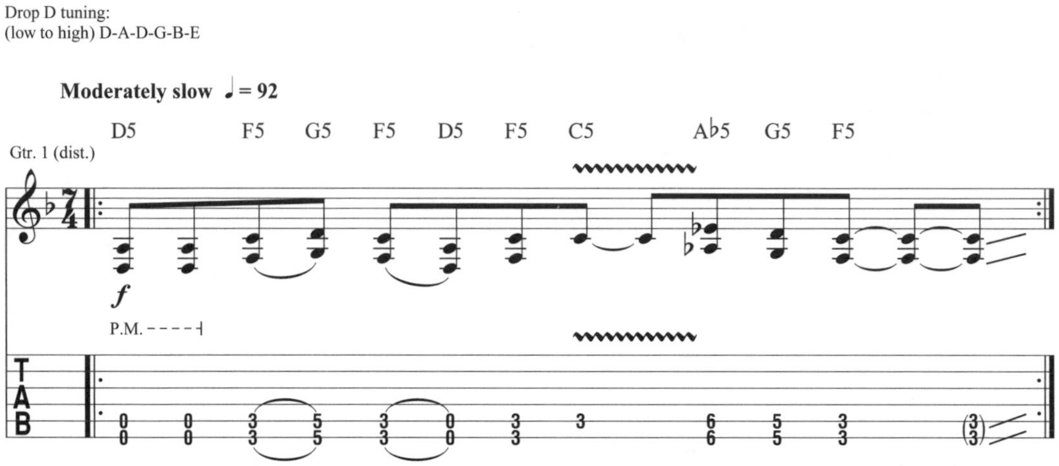

Photograph

Words and Music by Joseph Elliott, Stephen Maynard Clark, Peter Andrew Willis, Richard Savage, Richard John Cyril Allen and R.J. Lange

ARTIST: Def Leppard

ALBUM: *Pyromania*

YEAR: 1983

GUITARISTS: Steve Clark, Pete Willis

TIP: Although you *could* play the riff without shifting fret-hand positions, it's best to play the opening E5 with your middle finger on string 4 and ring finger on string 3, placing your index down one fret behind your ring finger, so you're all set for the subsequent B dyad. For the A5 in bar 2, move your index finger back to the 7th fret and barre across strings 4–3, while placing your ring finger at the 9th fret on string 3. Next, lift your ring finger and place your pinky on the 10th fret on string 2 for the D5/A chord. Use all downstrokes for the riff. The tuning legend says to tune down 1/2 step, but this is only necessary if you want to play along with the recording.

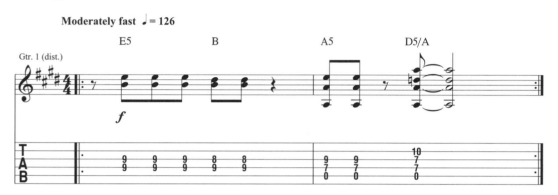

Purple Haze

Words and Music by Jimi Hendrix

ARTIST: The Jimi Hendrix Experience

ALBUM: *Are You Experienced?*

YEAR: 1967

GUITARIST: Jimi Hendrix

TRIVIA: "Purple Haze" marks the vinyl debut of the Octavia pedal, which is prominently featured in the guitar solo and outro. Tracked at De Lane Lea and Olympic Studios in London in early 1967, it was released as a single in the U.S. on June 19, 1967—one day after Jimi's guitar-scorching performance at the Monterey Pop Festival.

Rebel, Rebel

Words and Music by David Bowie

ARTIST: David Bowie

ALBUM: *Diamond Dogs*

YEAR: 1974

GUITARIST: Alan Parker

TIP: To begin this riff, fret an open Dsus2 chord before playing the open D notes. While holding that shape, you'll next encounter the E/D dyad on beat 2. The D note here, though clearly sounded on the recording, is almost certainly incidental. Use an upstroke on the dyad, so that the E note gets the prominence it should have. The next helpful tip is when you encounter the E triad on the "and" of beat 4, be sure to fret the 2nd-fret E note on string 4 as well, since you'll need it later in the riff. This will also set you up to comfortably use your ring finger for the pull-off on beat 3 of bar 2.

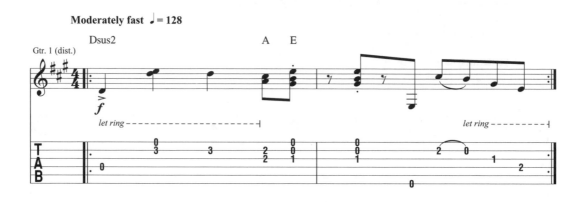

Rhiannon

Words and Music by Stevie Nicks

ARTIST: Fleetwood Mac

ALBUM: *Fleetwood Mac*

YEAR: 1975

GUITARIST: Lindsey Buckingham

TIP: The trickiest part of Lindsey Buckingham's fingerstyle riff is maintaining a steady rhythm while coordinating the thumb-picked bass notes and finger-plucked dyads, so practice the riff in chunks, starting slowly and working up to speed. For the Am-based fingerings, use index and middle fingers on strings 2 and 3, respectively, for the first two dyads, then your middle and ring fingers for the 5th-fret dyad in bar 1, as well as the on the 2nd-fret dyad on the "and" of beat 2 in bar 2. For the F-based chords in bars 3–4, note that you'll need to wrap your fret-hand thumb around the neck to fret the low F. For the dyads, simply assign your index, middle, and ring fingers to strings 2, 3, and 4, respectively.

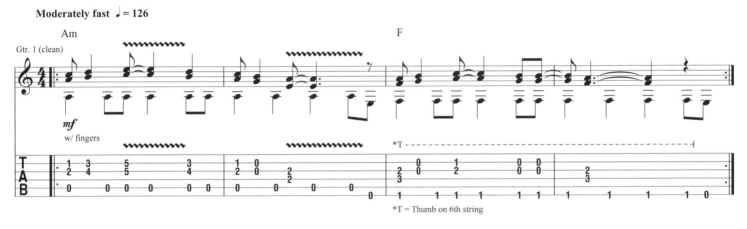

Rollin' Stone (Catfish Blues)

Words and Music by McKinley Morganfield

Artist: Muddy Waters

Album: *The Best of Muddy Waters*

Year: 1958

Guitarist: Muddy Waters

Tip: So influential is this gut-bucket blues riff that the world's greatest rock 'n' roll band named themselves for it. Set in the key of E in open position, Waters milked the major-minor-3rd (G#–G) rub)—defining sound of the blues—for all it's worth. Use your middle finger to perform the G-string bends and your ring finger on the low G.

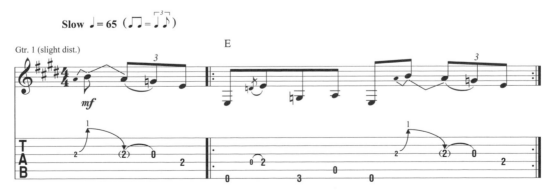

Satch Boogie

By Joe Satriani

ARTIST: Joe Satriani

ALBUM: *Surfing with the Alien*

YEAR: 1987

GUITARIST: Joe Satriani

TIP: Played at a scorching 215 beats per minute, you're going to need some time to build this one up to speed. The opening bar is played in 3rd position with your index and ring fingers. When you get to the downbeat of bar 2, it may be tempting to stay in 3rd position and play that legato triplet with your ring and pinky fingers, but Satriani actually shifts up to 5th position there and uses his index and middle fingers, and then quickly shifts his index finger back to the 2nd fret for the A note on string 3. At bar 3, you'll start in 2nd position with your ring finger on the 4th-fret C# (string 5), then for beat 2, slide it up one fret and grab the 4th-fret F# with your middle finger.

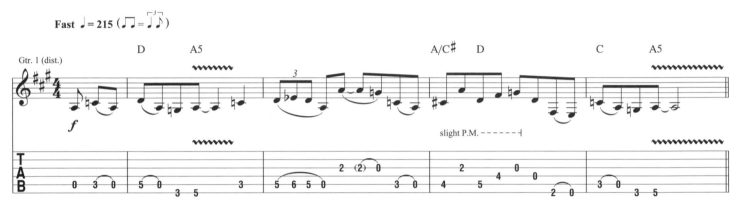

Seven Nation Army

Words and Music by Jack White

ARTIST: The White Stripes

ALBUM: *Elephant*

YEAR: 2002

GUITARIST: Jack White

TIP: To play this simple yet anthemic riff, use your fret hand's ring finger on frets 7 and 10, and index finger on frets 5, 3, and 2. Note the *quarter-note triplets* in bars 1 and 3. This is a tricky rhythm for most players. You need to play three notes with equal duration in the space of just two beats. The best way to visualize this rhythm is to split the quarter-note triplet into two eighth-note triplets, and then play those three notes on the italicized subdivisions like this: "*three*-and-*uh*, four-*and*-uh."

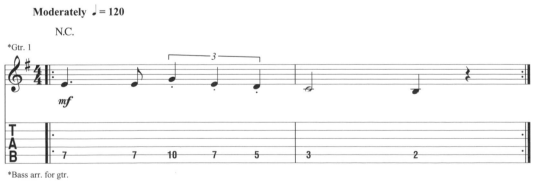

Smoke on the Water

Words and Music by Ritchie Blackmore, Ian Gillan, Roger Glover, Jon Lord and Ian Paice

ARTIST: Deep Purple

ALBUM: *Machine Head*

YEAR: 1972

GUITARIST: Ritchie Blackmore

TIP: This may very well be the most recognizable and most-played guitar riff in history. The riff gets much of its muscle from Blackmore's use of inverted power chords, or 4ths intervals, in its composition. Use a ring-finger barre for all the chords at the 5th and 6th frets and an index-finger barre for the Bb5 at the 3rd fret. Watch the staccato markings (small dot immediately below the notehead), as these indicate that the chord should be played "short;" that is, not allowed to ring for its full rhythmic duration.

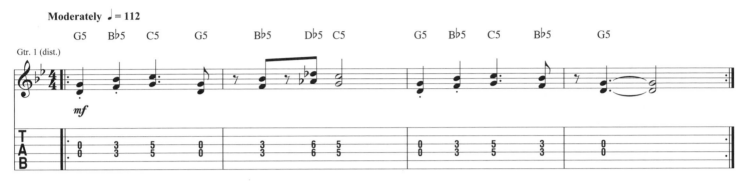

Snow (Hey Oh)

Words and Music by Anthony Kiedis, Flea, John Frusciante and Chad Smith

ARTIST: Red Hot Chili Peppers

ALBUM: *Stadium Arcadium*

YEAR: 2006

GUITARIST: John Frusciante

TIP: The Red Hot Chili Peppers are known for funky, syncopated riffs, but "Snow (Hey Oh)" relies on a well-crafted chord progression played in arpeggiated fashion with smooth legato embellishments to catch the ear. Somewhat rare in rock guitar, guitarist John Frusciante employs C-shape arpeggios for the E, B, and F# chords in bars 1–2. For these, you'll play the lowest root note of the chord with your fret hand's pinky finger, with your ring and index fingers grabbing the next two notes in the chord. Doing so also sets you up well for the hammer-on/pull-off combination in each chord.

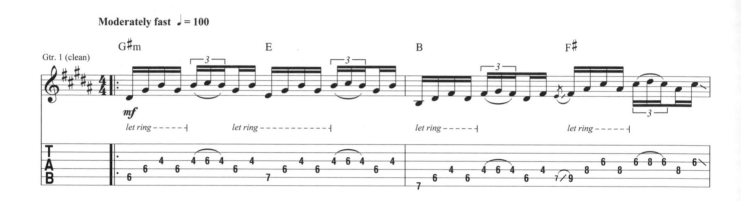

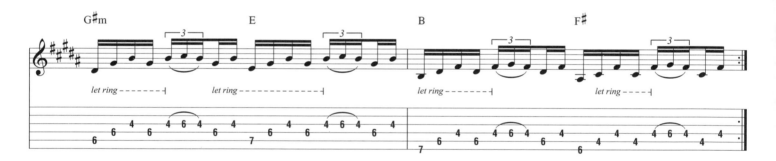

Sunday Bloody Sunday

Words and Music by U2

ARTIST: U2

ALBUM: *War*

YEAR: 1983

GUITARIST: The Edge

TIP: Guitarist Dave "The Edge" Evans arpeggiates the Bm–D–G6 progression in primarily a steady eighth-note rhythm, using about as efficient a fingering as you can get. To begin, fret an open D major chord shape in 2nd position, but then add your pinky finger to the 3rd string at the 4th fret, to get the Bm triad. Next, simply lift your pinky for the D major triad. And finally, while keeping your ring finger on the 2nd-string D note, lift your index and middle fingers, and you're set for the G6. For picking direction, play the first two notes of each arpeggio with downstrokes and the second two with upstrokes.

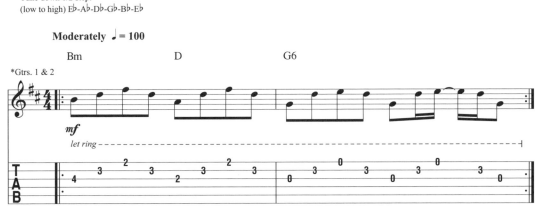

Sunshine of Your Love

Words and Music by Eric Clapton, Jack Bruce and Pete Brown

ARTIST: Cream

ALBUM: *Disraeli Gears*

Year: 1967

GUITARIST: Eric Clapton

TIP: "Sunshine of Your Love" is in the key of D, and this riff is straight out of the D blues scale (D–F–G–A–C). Start the riff with your fret hand in 10th position, ring finger on the 4th-string D note (12th fret). You'll stay in this position for all of measure 1 and the first note of measure 2. Then, quickly shift down two frets, to 8th position, and grab that 10th-fret D on the 6th string with your ring finger. In theory, you could stay in 10th position for the entire riff and play the 8th-fret F note on beat 3 of measure 2 instead at the 13th fret on the 6th string, but the vibrato on that F note is better achieved the way Clapton played it—as written.

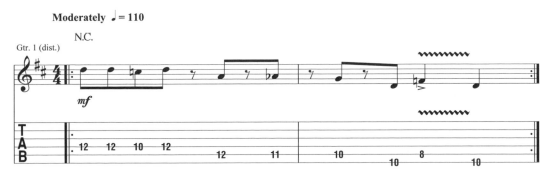

Susie-Q

Words and Music by Dale Hawkins, Stan Lewis and Eleanor Broadwater

ARTIST: Creedence Clearwater Revival

ALBUM: *Creedence Clearwater Revival*

YEAR: 1968

GUITARISTS: John Fogerty, Tom Fogerty

TIP: "Susie-Q," originally recorded by Dale Hawkins with James Burton on guitar, is formed from the E minor pentatonic scale (E–G–A–B–D) and played fingerstyle, with your thumb picking all the open low E notes. For the melody notes, use your pick hand's middle finger on the 2nd-string D note (3rd fret) and your index finger for remainder. As for fretting recommendations, use your ring finger on the 3rd-fret notes and your middle finger on the 2nd-fret ones.

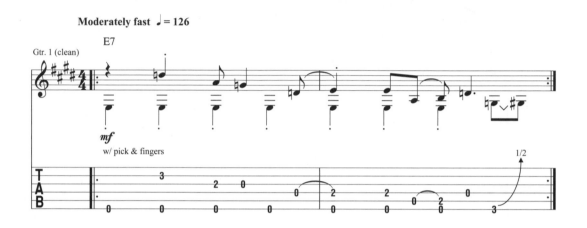

Sweet Child o' Mine

Words and Music by W. Axl Rose, Slash, Izzy Stradlin', Duff McKagan and Steven Adler

ARTIST: Guns N' Roses

ALBUM: *Appetite for Destruction*

YEAR: 1987

GUITARIST: Slash

TIP: If you look closely at the riff, it's the exact same pattern in every measure, except the starting note changes every two bars. There are several ways you can approach the fingering, but the most efficient is a simple one-finger-per-fret strategy, with your index on all 12th-fret notes, ring finger on all 14th-fret notes, and your pinky on all 15th-fret notes. Use alternate picking throughout, except for the A–G notes on beat 2 of each bar; using consecutive downstrokes there will allow for an easier jump up to the 15th-fret G on string 1 that follows.

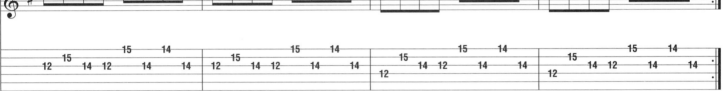

Sweet Home Alabama

Words and Music by Ronnie Van Zant, Ed King and Gary Rossington

ARTIST: Lynyrd Skynyrd

ALBUM: *Second Helping*

YEAR: 1974

GUITARISTS: Allen Collins, Gary Rossington, Ed King

TIP: Turn it up! "Sweet Home Alabama" is one of the finest examples of the I–VII–IV chord progression—in this case, D–C–G—popular in rock music. There are a couple of key points to note here. First, as you play through the chords, you should notice that the D note at the 3rd fret of string 2 is common to every chord. Therefore, you can keep your ring finger planted on that note through the entire D–C–G portion, not including the fills. Second, you'll see that on each change to the Csus2 and G chords, the root notes surround their respective open string. That open string is more of a *ghost* note than a clearly plucked one, so be sure to give the C and G root notes a bit more gusto.

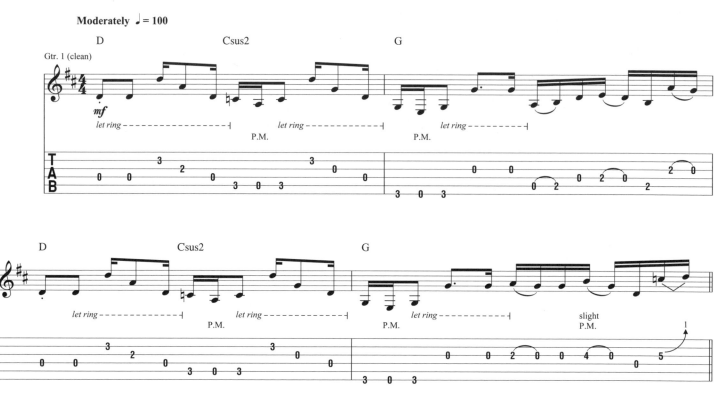

Sweet Home Chicago

Words and Music by Robert Johnson

ARTIST: The Blues Brothers

ALBUM: *The Blues Brothers* Original Soundtrack Recording

YEAR: 1980

GUITARIST: Steve Cropper, Matt "Guitar" Murphy

TIP: "Sweet Home Chicago" is one of the landmark Delta blues treasures written by the great Robert Johnson. The opening riff features Matt Murphy's take on Johnson's turnaround. Slide into the opening double stop on frets 16 and 15 with the ring and middle fingers respectively. On beat 3 of measures 1 and 2, use your index finger to partially barre the 14th fret on strings 2 and 3; use the same finger to barre the 12th fret on beat 4 of measure 2. Be sure to let the triplets ring on the walk down to the E and B9 chords.

Ticket to Ride

Words and Music by John Lennon and Paul McCartney

ARTIST: The Beatles

ALBUM: *Help!*

YEAR: 1965

GUITARISTS: George Harrison, John Lennon

TIP: This riff is based on an open A chord, with a suspended 2nd (B) providing the perfect amount of harmonic momentum. The fretted A note (string 3) and open E note serve as drones, lending the riff an almost Indian-like sound—one which the band would explore much more in depth on later recordings. And the quarter-note triplets (three quarter notes squeezed equally into the space of two quarter-note beats) fuel the riff rhythmically. To begin, fret the partial A chord using your middle finger on string 3 and ring finger on string 2, lifting the latter as needed for the Asus2 chord.

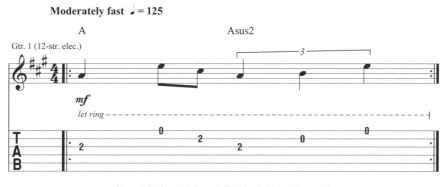

The Trooper

Words and Music by Steve Harris

ARTIST: Iron Maiden

ALBUM: *Piece of Mind*

YEAR: 1983

GUITARISTS: Dave Murray, Adrian Smith

TIP: Set in heavy metal's favorite key, E minor, the primary motif of this riff is the repeating diatonic (i.e., "in key") pattern across the E5, D5, and C5 chords, where the root is firmly stated in eighth notes and then followed by a pull-off lick. For the E5 and D5 versions, use your ring finger on the root notes, pulling off to your index finger two frets below. For C5, use your middle finger on the roots and to execute the pull-off. This requires quick shifts down the neck, so take your time to transition as smoothly as possible, and then build up to speed. For the eighth-note phrase on beats 3 and 4 of bar 2, quickly shift up to 5th position, where your index finger will cover the 5th-fret notes, leaving your ring finger in place on the 7th fret to start it all over again.

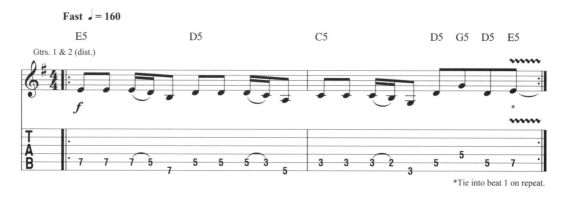

*Tie into beat 1 on repeat.

Walk This Way

Words and Music by Steven Tyler and Joe Perry

ARTIST: *Aerosmith*

ALBUM: *Toys in the Attic*

YEAR: 1975

GUITARISTS: *Joe Perry, Brad Whitford*

TIP: Joe Perry's enduring riff is based in the E blues scale (E–G–A–B♭–B–D). For the initial walk up from A–B♭–B, use your index and middle fingers, then rolling your middle finger over to the 4th string to grab the E note at the 2nd fret. Next, Perry employs a slight rhythmic displacement, restating the phrase on the second 16th note of beat 2—make sure you recognize that 16th rest. On beat 4, lay your fret hand's fingers across the lowest two strings for those muted notes. It's fine if you hit both strings, as long as they're properly muted. On beat 4 of bar 2, make sure you hit that E note as staccato, so it doesn't ring for its full duration. Use alternate picking throughout, except for consecutive downstrokes on those muted notes in bar 1.

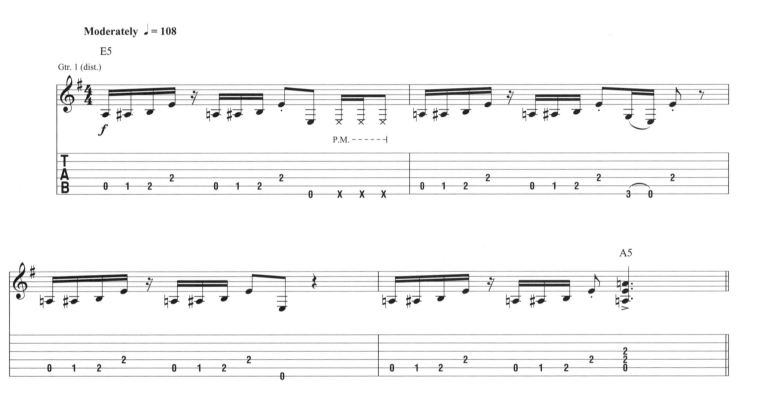

Wish You Were Here

Words and Music by Roger Waters and David Gilmour

ARTIST: Pink Floyd

ALBUM: *Wish You Were Here*

YEAR: 1975

GUITARIST: David Gilmour

TIP: David Gilmour created a masterpiece with the main riff to "Wish You Were Here," as well as a master class in using common tones. Although you're going to play two different chords (Em7, G) during this riff, you'll keep your fret hand's ring and pinky fingers anchored on the D and G notes at the 3rd fret of the B and E strings, respectively, throughout. Your middle finger only need worry about that low G note (3rd fret, 6th string), and your index finger will do all the work.

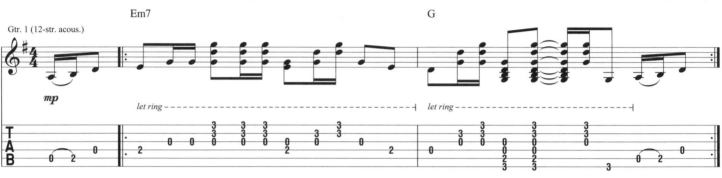

Working Man

Words and Music by Geddy Lee and Alex Lifeson

ARTIST: Rush

ALBUM: *Rush*

YEAR: 1974

GUITARIST: Alex Lifeson

TIP: This song is in the key of E major, but the riff features notes from the E minor scale (E–F♯–G–A–B–C–D). In fact, Alex Lifeson pretty much relies on the E minor scale for all his extensive soloing. After playing the opening E5 power chord, move up to 3rd position, so that your ring finger grabs both the 5th-fret D (string 5) and the 5th-fret A (string 6). In bar 2, make that same shift to 3rd position, so that your index finger frets the 3rd-fret C (string 5). Note the "loping" rhythm of beat 1 in each measure. It's a dotted eighth followed by a 16th note, so if you subdivide the beat into four 16th notes, the first E5 chord is held for the first three 16ths.

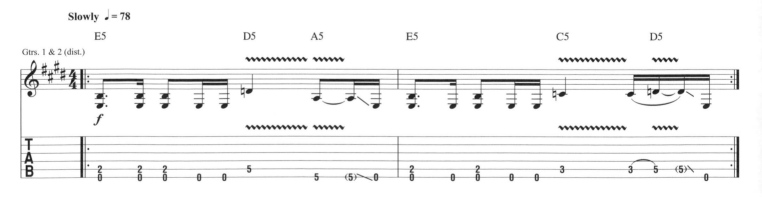

GUITAR NOTATION LEGEND

Guitar music can be notated three different ways: on a *musical staff*, in *tablature*, and in *rhythm slashes*.

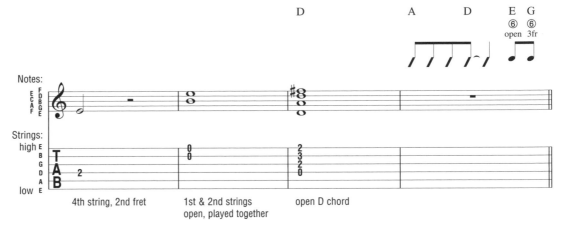

RHYTHM SLASHES are written above the staff. Strum chords in the rhythm indicated. Use the chord diagrams found at the top of the first page of the transcription for the appropriate chord voicings. Round noteheads indicate single notes.

THE MUSICAL STAFF shows pitches and rhythms and is divided by bar lines into measures. Pitches are named after the first seven letters of the alphabet.

TABLATURE graphically represents the guitar fingerboard. Each horizontal line represents a string, and each number represents a fret.

4th string, 2nd fret   1st & 2nd strings open, played together   open D chord

Definitions for Special Guitar Notation

HALF-STEP BEND: Strike the note and bend up 1/2 step.

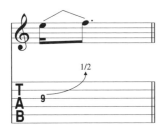

WHOLE-STEP BEND: Strike the note and bend up one step.

GRACE NOTE BEND: Strike the note and immediately bend up as indicated.

SLIGHT (MICROTONE) BEND: Strike the note and bend up 1/4 step.

BEND AND RELEASE: Strike the note and bend up as indicated, then release back to the original note. Only the first note is struck.

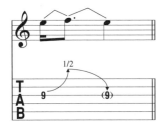

PRE-BEND: Bend the note as indicated, then strike it.

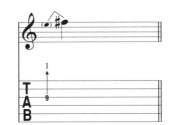

PRE-BEND AND RELEASE: Bend the note as indicated. Strike it and release the bend back to the original note.

UNISON BEND: Strike the two notes simultaneously and bend the lower note up to the pitch of the higher.

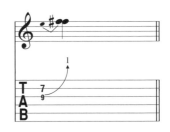

VIBRATO: The string is vibrated by rapidly bending and releasing the note with the fretting hand.

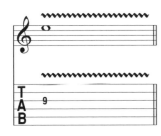

WIDE VIBRATO: The pitch is varied to a greater degree by vibrating with the fretting hand.

HAMMER-ON: Strike the first (lower) note with one finger, then sound the higher note (on the same string) with another finger by fretting it without picking.

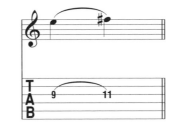

PULL-OFF: Place both fingers on the notes to be sounded. Strike the first note and without picking, pull the finger off to sound the second (lower) note.

LEGATO SLIDE: Strike the first note and then slide the same fret-hand finger up or down to the second note. The second note is not struck.

SHIFT SLIDE: Same as legato slide, except the second note is struck.

TRILL: Very rapidly alternate between the notes indicated by continuously hammering on and pulling off.

TAPPING: Hammer ("tap") the fret indicated with the pick-hand index or middle finger and pull off to the note fretted by the fret hand.

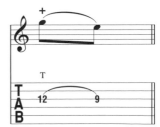

NATURAL HARMONIC: Strike the note while the fret-hand lightly touches the string directly over the fret indicated.

PINCH HARMONIC: The note is fretted normally and a harmonic is produced by adding the edge of the thumb or the tip of the index finger of the pick hand to the normal pick attack.

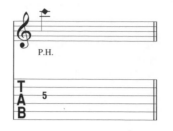

HARP HARMONIC: The note is fretted normally and a harmonic is produced by gently resting the pick hand's index finger directly above the indicated fret (in parentheses) while the pick hand's thumb or pick assists by plucking the appropriate string.

PICK SCRAPE: The edge of the pick is rubbed down (or up) the string, producing a scratchy sound.

MUFFLED STRINGS: A percussive sound is produced by laying the fret hand across the string(s) without depressing, and striking them with the pick hand.

PALM MUTING: The note is partially muted by the pick hand lightly touching the string(s) just before the bridge.

RAKE: Drag the pick across the strings indicated with a single motion.

TREMOLO PICKING: The note is picked as rapidly and continuously as possible.

ARPEGGIATE: Play the notes of the chord indicated by quickly rolling them from bottom to top.

VIBRATO BAR DIVE AND RETURN: The pitch of the note or chord is dropped a specified number of steps (in rhythm), then returned to the original pitch.

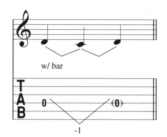

VIBRATO BAR SCOOP: Depress the bar just before striking the note, then quickly release the bar.

VIBRATO BAR DIP: Strike the note and then immediately drop a specified number of steps, then release back to the original pitch.

Additional Musical Definitions

(accent)	• Accentuate note (play it louder).	
(accent)	• Accentuate note with great intensity.	
(staccato)	• Play the note short.	
⊓	• Downstroke	
V	• Upstroke	
D.S. al Coda	• Go back to the sign (𝄋), then play until the measure marked "*To Coda*," then skip to the section labelled "**Coda**."	
D.C. al Fine	• Go back to the beginning of the song and play until the measure marked "*Fine*" (end).	

Rhy. Fig. • Label used to recall a recurring accompaniment pattern (usually chordal).

Riff • Label used to recall composed, melodic lines (usually single notes) which recur.

Fill • Label used to identify a brief melodic figure which is to be inserted into the arrangement.

Rhy. Fill • A chordal version of a Fill.

tacet • Instrument is silent (drops out).

• Repeat measures between signs.

• When a repeated section has different endings, play the first ending only the first time and the second ending only the second time.

NOTE: Tablature numbers in parentheses mean:
1. The note is being sustained over a system (note in standard notation is tied), or
2. The note is sustained, but a new articulation (such as a hammer-on, pull-off, slide or vibrato) begins, or
3. The note is a barely audible "ghost" note (note in standard notation is also in parentheses).

FIRST 50

Books in the First 50 series contain easy to intermediate arrangements for must-know songs. Each arrangement is simple and streamlined, yet still captures the essence of the tune.

First 50 Baroque Pieces
You Should Play on Guitar
Includes selections by Johann Sebastian Bach, Robert de Visée, Ernst Gottlieb Baron, Santiago de Murcia, Antonio Vivaldi, Sylvius Leopold Weiss, and more.
00322567.................................$14.99

First 50 Bluegrass Solos
You Should Play on Guitar
I Am a Man of Constant Sorrow • Long Journey Home • Molly and Tenbrooks • Old Joe Clark • Rocky Top • Salty Dog Blues • and more.
00298574.................................$16.99

First 50 Blues Songs
You Should Play on Guitar
All Your Love (I Miss Loving) • Bad to the Bone • Born Under a Bad Sign • Dust My Broom • Hoodoo Man Blues • Little Red Rooster • Love Struck Baby • Pride and Joy • Smoking Gun • Still Got the Blues • The Thrill Is Gone • You Shook Me • and more.
00235790.................................$17.99

First 50 Blues Turnarounds
You Should Play on Guitar
You'll learn cool turnarounds in the styles of these jazz legends: John Lee Hooker, Robert Johnson, Joe Pass, Jimmy Rogers, Hubert Sumlin, Stevie Ray Vaughan, T-Bone Walker, Muddy Waters, and more.
00277469.................................$14.99

First 50 Chords
You Should Play on Guitar
American Pie • Back in Black • Brown Eyed Girl • Landslide • Let It Be • Riptide • Summer of '69 • Take Me Home, Country Roads • Won't Get Fooled Again • You've Got a Friend • and more.
00300255 Guitar.................................$12.99

First 50 Classical Pieces
You Should Play on Guitar
Includes compositions by J.S. Bach, Augustin Barrios, Matteo Carcassi, Domenico Scarlatti, Fernando Sor, Francisco Tárrega, Robert de Visée, Antonio Vivaldi and many more.
00155414.................................$16.99

First 50 Folk Songs
You Should Play on Guitar
Amazing Grace • Down by the Riverside • Home on the Range • I've Been Working on the Railroad • Kumbaya • Man of Constant Sorrow • Oh! Susanna • This Little Light of Mine • When the Saints Go Marching In • The Yellow Rose of Texas • and more.
00235868.................................$16.99

First 50 Guitar Duets
You Should Play
Chopsticks • Clocks • Eleanor Rigby • Game of Thrones Theme • Hallelujah • Linus and Lucy (from *A Charlie Brown Christmas*) • Memory (from *Cats*) • Over the Rainbow (from *The Wizard of Oz*) • Star Wars (Main Theme) • What a Wonderful World • You Raise Me Up • and more.
00319706.................................$14.99

First 50 Jazz Standards
You Should Play on Guitar
All the Things You Are • Body and Soul • Don't Get Around Much Anymore • Fly Me to the Moon (In Other Words) • The Girl from Ipanema (Garota De Ipanema) • I Got Rhythm • Laura • Misty • Night and Day • Satin Summertime • When I Fall in Love • and more.
00198594 Solo Guitar.................................$16.99

First 50 Kids' Songs
You Should Play on Guitar
Do-Re-Mi • Hakuna Matata • Let It Go • My Favorite Things • Puff the Magic Dragon • Take Me Out to the Ball Game • Won't You Be My Neighbor? (It's a Beautiful Day in the Neighborhood) • and more.
00300500.................................$15.99

First 50 Licks
You Should Play on Guitar
Licks presented include the styles of legendary guitarists like Eric Clapton, Buddy Guy, Jimi Hendrix, B.B. King, Randy Rhoads, Carlos Santana, Stevie Ray Vaughan and many more.
00278875 Book/Online Audio.................................$14.99

First 50 Riffs
You Should Play on Guitar
All Right Now • Back in Black • Barracuda • Carry on Wayward Son • Crazy Train • La Grange • Layla • Seven Nation Army • Smoke on the Water • Sunday Bloody Sunday • Sunshine of Your Love • Sweet Home Alabama • Working Man • and more.
00277366.................................$14.99

First 50 Rock Songs You Should
Play on Electric Guitar
All Along the Watchtower • Beat It • Brown Eyed Girl • Cocaine • Detroit Rock City • Hallelujah • (I Can't Get No) Satisfaction • Oh, Pretty Woman • Pride and Joy • Seven Nation Army • Should I Stay or Should I Go • Smells like Teen Spirit • Smoke on the Water • When I Come Around • You Really Got Me • and more.
00131159.................................$15.99

First 50 Songs by the Beatles You
Should Play on Guitar
All You Need Is Love • Blackbird • Come Together • Eleanor Rigby • Hey Jude • I Want to Hold Your Hand • Let It Be • Ob-La-Di, Ob-La-Da • She Loves You • Twist and Shout • Yellow Submarine • Yesterday • and more.
00295323.................................$19.99

First 50 Songs
You Should Fingerpick on Guitar
Annie's Song • Blackbird • The Boxer • Classical Gas • Dust in the Wind • Fire and Rain • Greensleeves • Road Trippin' • Shape of My Heart • Tears in Heaven • Time in a Bottle • Vincent (Starry Starry Night) • and more.
00149269.................................$16.99

First 50 Songs You Should
Play on 12-String Guitar
California Dreamin' • Closer to the Heart • Free Fallin' • Give a Little Bit • Hotel California • Leaving on a Jet Plane • Life by the Drop • Over the Hills and Far Away • Solsbury Hill • Space Oddity • Wish You Were Here • You Wear It Well • and more.
00287559.................................$15.99

First 50 Songs You Should Play on
Acoustic Guitar
Against the Wind • Boulevard of Broken Dreams • Champagne Supernova • Every Rose Has Its Thorn • Fast Car • Free Fallin' • Layla • Let Her Go • Mean • One • Ring of Fire • Signs • Stairway to Heaven • Trouble • Wagon Wheel • Yellow • Yesterday • and more.
00131209.................................$16.99

First 50 Songs
You Should Play on Bass
Blister in the Sun • I Got You (I Feel Good) • Livin' on a Prayer • Low Rider • Money • Monkey Wrench • My Generation • Roxanne • Should I Stay or Should I Go • Uptown Funk • What's Going On • With or Without You • Yellow • and more.
00149189.................................$16.99

First 50 Songs
You Should Play on Solo Guitar
Africa • All of Me • Blue Skies • California Dreamin' • Change the World • Crazy • Dream a Little Dream of Me • Every Breath You Take • Hallelujah • Wonderful Tonight • Yesterday • You Raise Me Up • Your Song • and more.
00288843.................................$17.99

First 50 Songs
You Should Strum on Guitar
American Pie • Blowin' in the Wind • Daughter • Hey, Soul Sister • Home • I Will Wait • Losing My Religion • Mrs. Robinson • No Woman No Cry • Peaceful Easy Feeling • Rocky Mountain High • Sweet Caroline • Teardrops on My Guitar • Wonderful Tonight • and more.
00148996 Guitar.................................$16.99

HAL•LEONARD®
www.halleonard.com

Prices, contents and availability subject to change without notice.

This series features simplified arrangements with notes, tab, chord charts, and strum and pick patterns.

MIXED FOLIOS

00702287	Acoustic	$19.99
00702002	Acoustic Rock Hits for Easy Guitar	$15.99
00702166	All-Time Best Guitar Collection	$19.99
00702232	Best Acoustic Songs for Easy Guitar	$16.99
00119835	Best Children's Songs	$16.99
00703055	The Big Book of Nursery Rhymes & Children's Songs	$16.99
00698978	Big Christmas Collection	$19.99
00702394	Bluegrass Songs for Easy Guitar	$15.99
00289632	Bohemian Rhapsody	$19.99
00703387	Celtic Classics	$16.99
00224808	Chart Hits of 2016-2017	$14.99
00267383	Chart Hits of 2017-2018	$14.99
00334293	Chart Hits of 2019-2020	$16.99
00403479	Chart Hits of 2021-2022	$16.99
00702149	Children's Christian Songbook	$9.99
00702028	Christmas Classics	$8.99
00101779	Christmas Guitar	$14.99
00702141	Classic Rock	$8.95
00159642	Classical Melodies	$12.99
00253933	Disney/Pixar's Coco	$16.99
00702203	CMT's 100 Greatest Country Songs	$34.99
00702283	The Contemporary Christian Collection	$16.99

00196954	Contemporary Disney	$19.99
00702239	Country Classics for Easy Guitar	$24.99
00702257	Easy Acoustic Guitar Songs	$17.99
00702041	Favorite Hymns for Easy Guitar	$12.99
00222701	Folk Pop Songs	$17.99
00126894	Frozen	$14.99
00333922	Frozen 2	$14.99
00702286	Glee	$16.99
00702160	The Great American Country Songbook	$19.99
00702148	Great American Gospel for Guitar	$14.99
00702050	Great Classical Themes for Easy Guitar	$9.99
00275088	The Greatest Showman	$17.99
00148030	Halloween Guitar Songs	$14.99
00702273	Irish Songs	$14.99
00192503	Jazz Classics for Easy Guitar	$16.99
00702275	Jazz Favorites for Easy Guitar	$17.99
00702274	Jazz Standards for Easy Guitar	$19.99
00702162	Jumbo Easy Guitar Songbook	$24.99
00232285	La La Land	$16.99
00702258	Legends of Rock	$14.99
00702189	MTV's 100 Greatest Pop Songs	$34.99
00702272	1950s Rock	$16.99
00702271	1960s Rock	$16.99
00702270	1970s Rock	$24.99
00702269	1980s Rock	$16.99

00702268	1990s Rock	$24.99
00369043	Rock Songs for Kids	$14.99
00109725	Once	$14.99
00702187	Selections from O Brother Where Art Thou?	$19.99
00702178	100 Songs for Kids	$16.99
00702515	Pirates of the Caribbean	$17.99
00702125	Praise and Worship for Guitar	$14.99
00287930	Songs from *A Star Is Born, The Greatest Showman, La La Land,* and More Movie Musicals	$16.99
00702285	Southern Rock Hits	$12.99
00156420	Star Wars Music	$16.99
00121535	30 Easy Celtic Guitar Solos	$16.99
00244654	Top Hits of 2017	$14.99
00283786	Top Hits of 2018	$14.99
00302269	Top Hits of 2019	$14.99
00355779	Top Hits of 2020	$14.99
00374083	Top Hits of 2021	$16.99
00702294	Top Worship Hits	$17.99
00702255	VH1's 100 Greatest Hard Rock Songs	$34.99
00702175	VH1's 100 Greatest Songs of Rock and Roll	$34.99
00702253	Wicked	$12.99

ARTIST COLLECTIONS

00702267	AC/DC for Easy Guitar	$16.99
00156221	Adele – 25	$16.99
00396889	Adele – 30	$19.99
00702040	Best of the Allman Brothers	$16.99
00702865	J.S. Bach for Easy Guitar	$15.99
00702169	Best of The Beach Boys	$16.99
00702292	The Beatles — 1	$22.99
00125796	Best of Chuck Berry	$16.99
00702201	The Essential Black Sabbath	$15.99
00702250	blink-182 — Greatest Hits	$17.99
02501615	Zac Brown Band — The Foundation	$17.99
02501621	Zac Brown Band — You Get What You Give	$16.99
00702043	Best of Johnny Cash	$17.99
00702090	Eric Clapton's Best	$16.99
00702086	Eric Clapton — from the Album Unplugged	$17.99
00702202	The Essential Eric Clapton	$17.99
00702053	Best of Patsy Cline	$17.99
00222697	Very Best of Coldplay – 2nd Edition	$17.99
00702229	The Very Best of Creedence Clearwater Revival	$16.99
00702145	Best of Jim Croce	$16.99
00702278	Crosby, Stills & Nash	$12.99
14042809	Bob Dylan	$15.99
00702276	Fleetwood Mac — Easy Guitar Collection	$17.99
00139462	The Very Best of Grateful Dead	$16.99
00702136	Best of Merle Haggard	$16.99
00702227	Jimi Hendrix — Smash Hits	$19.99
00702288	Best of Hillsong United	$12.99
00702236	Best of Antonio Carlos Jobim	$15.99

00702245	Elton John — Greatest Hits 1970–2002	$19.99
00129855	Jack Johnson	$17.99
00702204	Robert Johnson	$16.99
00702234	Selections from Toby Keith — 35 Biggest Hits	$12.95
00702003	Kiss	$16.99
00702216	Lynyrd Skynyrd	$17.99
00702182	The Essential Bob Marley	$16.99
00146081	Maroon 5	$14.99
00121925	Bruno Mars – Unorthodox Jukebox	$12.99
00702248	Paul McCartney — All the Best	$14.99
00125484	The Best of MercyMe	$12.99
00702209	Steve Miller Band — Young Hearts (Greatest Hits)	$12.95
00124167	Jason Mraz	$15.99
00702096	Best of Nirvana	$16.99
00702211	The Offspring — Greatest Hits	$17.99
00138026	One Direction	$17.99
00702030	Best of Roy Orbison	$17.99
00702144	Best of Ozzy Osbourne	$14.99
00702279	Tom Petty	$17.99
00102911	Pink Floyd	$17.99
00702139	Elvis Country Favorites	$19.99
00702293	The Very Best of Prince	$19.99
00699415	Best of Queen for Guitar	$16.99
00109279	Best of R.E.M.	$14.99
00702208	Red Hot Chili Peppers — Greatest Hits	$17.99
00198960	The Rolling Stones	$17.99
00174793	The Very Best of Santana	$16.99
00702196	Best of Bob Seger	$16.99
00146046	Ed Sheeran	$17.99

00702252	Frank Sinatra — Nothing But the Best	$12.99
00702010	Best of Rod Stewart	$17.99
00702049	Best of George Strait	$17.99
00702259	Taylor Swift for Easy Guitar	$15.99
00359800	Taylor Swift – Easy Guitar Anthology	$24.99
00702260	Taylor Swift — Fearless	$14.99
00139727	Taylor Swift — 1989	$19.99
00115960	Taylor Swift — Red	$16.99
00253667	Taylor Swift — Reputation	$17.99
00702290	Taylor Swift — Speak Now	$16.99
00232849	Chris Tomlin Collection – 2nd Edition	$14.99
00702226	Chris Tomlin — See the Morning	$12.95
00148643	Train	$14.99
00702427	U2 — 18 Singles	$19.99
00702108	Best of Stevie Ray Vaughan	$17.99
00279005	The Who	$14.99
00702123	Best of Hank Williams	$15.99
00194548	Best of John Williams	$14.99
00702228	Neil Young — Greatest Hits	$17.99
00119133	Neil Young — Harvest	$14.99

Visit Hal Leonard online at **halleonard.com**